SOUPS & STARTERS

STARTERS

10 9 8 7 6 5 4 3 2 1

Publishing Manager: Fiona Schultz
Designer: Tania Gomes
Production Manager: Olga Dementiev
Printer: SNP/Leefung Printing Co. Ltd. (China)

Cover & internal photographs by Getty Images
Sweets photograph by NHIL

NEW HOLLAND PUBLISHERS
www.newholland.com.au